Beginning

GYMNASTICS

Gymnastics coaches Linda Wallenberg Bragg and Scott Gay and the following athletes were photographed for this book:
Jill Ames,
Tony Aretz,
Nikki Benedict,
Kristy Bowman,
Matt Bulger,
Heidi Cady,
Sara Dunphy,
R.J. Emery,
Beth Flaherty,
Andrew Gagner,
Andrew Hackman,
Christian Hyun,
Nicholas Johnson,
Lori Lehman,
Pat Nelson,
Adam Reichow,
Cathy Sohn,
Stacy Swigart,
Mark Tundel,
Kelli Ueland.

Beginning
GYMNASTICS

Julie Jensen

**Adapted from
Linda Wallenberg
Bragg's**
*Fundamental
Gymnastics*

**Photographs by
Andy King**

Lerner Publications Company ● Minneapolis

Photo Acknowledgments
Photographs are reproduced with the permission of:
p. 7, Scala/Art Resource, N.Y.; p. 8, The Bettmann
Archive; p. 9 (top), UPI/Bettmann; p. 9 (bottom),
ALLSPORT/Steve Powell; p. 10, ALLSPORT; p. 11,
ALLSPORT/Doug Pensinger; p. 14, ALLSPORT/
Tony Duffy; p. 63, ALLSPORT/Chris Cole; p. 74
(top), ALLSPORT/Gary M. Prior.

Copyright © 1995 by Lerner Publications Company

Library of Congress Cataloging-in-Publication Data

Jensen, Julie, 1957–
    Beginning gymnastics / Julie Jensen : adapted from Linda
Wallenberg Bragg's Fundamental gymnastics : photographs
by Andy King.
      p.   cm. — (Beginning sports)
    Includes bibliographical references and index.
    Summary: Covers the history, equipment and basic
techniques of gymnastics, as well as competitions and
performances.
    ISBN 0–8225–3503–3 (alk. paper)
    1. Gymnastics—Juvenile literature. [1. Gymnastics.]
I. King, Andy, ill. II. Bragg, Linda Wallenberg. Fundamental
gymnastics. III. Title. IV. Series.
GV461.J554 1995
796.44—dc20   95–7677
                                                   CIP
                                                   AC

Manufactured in the United States of America

1 2 3 4 5 6 - H/P - 00 99 98 97 96 95

Contents

How This Sport Got Started

Pretend you are standing on a piece of wood that is 4 inches wide. You lift your arms and jump. You curl up into a tight little ball. For a second you are upside down. Then you squeeze your ankles tight. In a flash, you are standing on that skinny piece of wood again. You did it! You did a gymnastic move.

Gymnasts use their strength and balance to do exciting moves. If flipping through the air sounds like fun to you, you would probably like to be a gymnast.

There are pictures of gymnasts on this old Greek vase.

Friedrich Jahn was a gymnastics teacher in Germany. He founded the first gymnastics club in 1811.

Gymnasts must combine athletic skills and moves with graceful dance movements. Some people think gymnastics is more of an art than a sport.

Gymnastics has been around for thousands of years. Most people believe that ancient Greeks began the sport of gymnastics. The Greeks loved to play sports. They held the first Olympic Games more than 2,000 years ago. There are pictures of athletes wrestling and tumbling on Greek paintings and vases.

Friedrich Jahn from Germany started the first gymnastics club. A gymnastics club is a group of gymnasts who train together. Jahn built an outdoor center for his gymnasts in 1811. He made equipment and taught his students moves on the equipment. Young gymnasts still learn in clubs.

Left, Mitsuo Tsukahara was a Japanese gymnast in the 1970s. Below, Bart Conner was on the United States team that won the gold medal at the 1984 Olympic Games.

Gymnastics became popular throughout the world between 1850 and 1900. Gymnasts used six pieces of equipment, called **apparatus:** the **parallel bars, horizontal bar, rings, pommel horse, vault,** and ropes. (They competed in rope climbing instead of the **floor exercise,** as gymnasts do now.) After the Olympic Games began again in 1896, gymnasts agreed on rules and standards.

Many children wanted to learn gymnastics after watching Olga Korbut in the 1972 Olympics.

At first, girls didn't learn gymnastics. Some people didn't think girls were strong enough to play any sports. However, women's gymnastics teams competed in the 1928 Olympics. Special equipment was built just for women's events. Women and girls got better and better at gymnastics. When the

1960 Olympics were shown on television, many people were amazed by the beauty of women's gymnastics.

By the 1970s, Olga Korbut from the Soviet Union, Nadia Comaneci from Romania, and Cathy Rigby from the United States were famous. Mary Lou Retton was a star for the United States in the 1980s.

This book will show you the basics of gymnastics. Learning gymnastics skills takes time and effort. Don't be discouraged if your first few flips flop. Find a good coach and do your best. Soon you'll be flying through the air with grace and confidence!

Dominique Dawes became a top gymnast in the 1990s.

BASICS

You can learn to do gymnastics. Many people are naturally strong or naturally flexible. The best gymnasts are both. A gymnast is usually a short, strong, light athlete.

At first, your coach will help you develop your coordination, balance, and flexibility. Beginning gymnasts work on pointing their toes and stretching their muscles. They start tumbling.

By the time gymnasts start school, they are often working on the gymnastics apparatus. Young gymnasts still spend much of their time tumbling.

What Does a Gymnast Wear?

When a gymnast is competing, he or she has to follow the rules of the group that is running the meet. Most clubs have specific rules about what a gymnast can wear. If a gymnast doesn't follow the rules, he or she will lose some points (called a deduction). Team members often wear the same type and color of uniform to show that they are a team.

Most coaches have rules about what gymnasts should wear when practicing. Most coaches don't allow gymnasts to wear T-shirts. Many coaches also insist that long hair be tied back. That way a gymnast's clothing doesn't get in the way when a coach is assisting a gymnast.

13

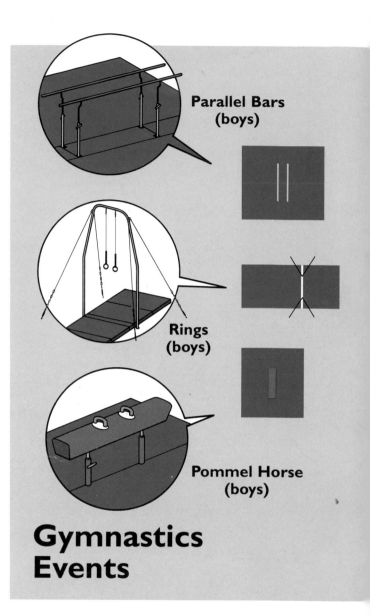

Parallel Bars (boys)

Rings (boys)

Pommel Horse (boys)

Gymnastics Events

Nadia Comaneci was a Romanian gymnast in the 1970s.

A Sport of Constant Change

*Gymnasts love to figure out new ways to perform old skills. They also enjoy thinking up completely new skills! New skills are usually named after the gymnasts who first perform them. For example, the **tsukahara** vault is named after a Japanese gymnast, Mitsuo Tsukahara. He was a famous gymnast in the 1970s. The **comaneci** dismount is named after Nadia Comaneci. She stunned the world with her amazing string of perfect routines.*

Male gymnasts compete in six events: floor exercise, vault, pommel horse, rings, parallel bars, and horizontal bar. Female gymnasts compete in four events: floor exercise, vault, **uneven parallel bars,** and **balance beam.**

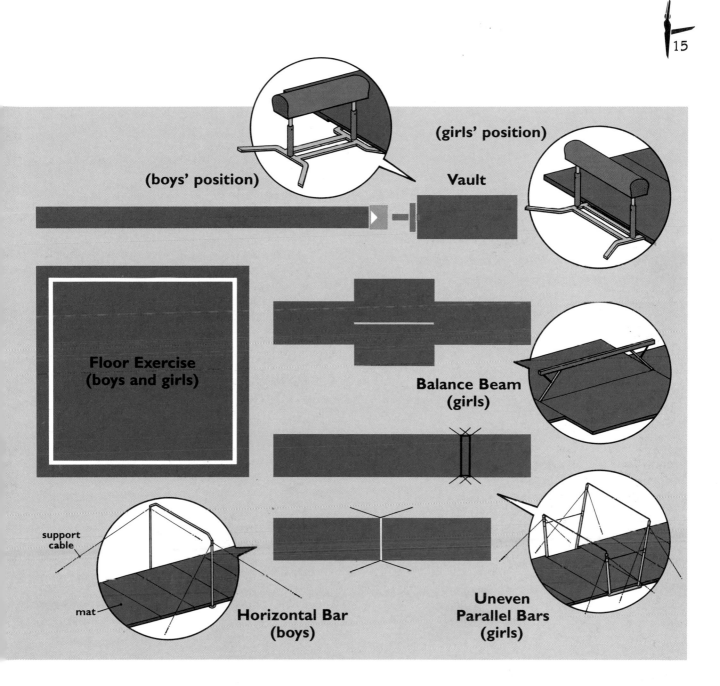

(boys' position)

(girls' position)

Vault

Floor Exercise
(boys and girls)

Balance Beam
(girls)

support
cable

mat

Horizontal Bar
(boys)

Uneven
Parallel Bars
(girls)

Boys and girls can learn some of the same skills even though their events are different. Boys and girls both compete in the floor exercise event. But the girls perform a floor routine to music. A girl's routine must have both tumbling and dance moves. The boys' floor routine isn't performed to music and doesn't include dance moves. Boys and girls both have a vault event. The girls vault over the horse sideways. The boys vault over the horse lengthwise. Boys and girls do the same vaults.

Boys' Events

● *Floor Exercise*

Mark is doing a basic floor exercise skill. It's called a **front handspring**.

Mark starts by standing up straight and reaching his arms to the ceiling. He runs and springs forward. Mark jumps up. His body is slightly arched and he's leaning forward. He puts his hands on the mat, about as far apart as his shoulders are. Then he kicks his legs

into the air and flips his legs over his head. He can land on one foot first and then the other, or he can land on both feet at the same time.

When gymnastics first started, gymnasts performed on bare floors or on very little padding. Now, a gymnastics floor has a layer of foam blocks or springs under at least one layer of wood. Another layer of thick foam is on top of the wood. A 40-feet by 40-feet piece of carpet is on top of the foam. This type of floor is called a rebound or **spring floor**. This floor helps keep the gymnast safe.

● *Vault*

The vault is also called the horse. The vault is a padded wooden frame 3 feet, 7 inches high. Boys use the vault positioned lengthwise.

The move a gymnast performs over the vault is also called a vault. A vault takes just four or five seconds to do.

A springboard is placed in front of the vault. Sometimes gymnasts use a mini-trampoline, as Christian is, instead of a springboard.

Christian begins his vault at the end of a long, cushioned runway. First, he runs and jumps on the mini-tramp. Then Christian touches the vault with his hands. This is called the **preflight**. He tries to touch the horse for very short amount of time.

Christian pushes off the vault and into the **postflight**. The postflight of most vaults has a flip or a **twist** or both. Then Christian lands on the protective landing mats.

● Pommel Horse

A pommel horse is a padded frame that is 3 feet, 7 inches high. A pommel horse has handles that are called pommels. A gymnast grips the pommels while he swings from side to side and forward and back. He has to let go of the pommels and then re-grasp them as he moves. Christian, at left, is beginning to learn how to move on the pommel horse.

Andrew, below, is practicing **circles** on a piece of equipment called a mushroom.

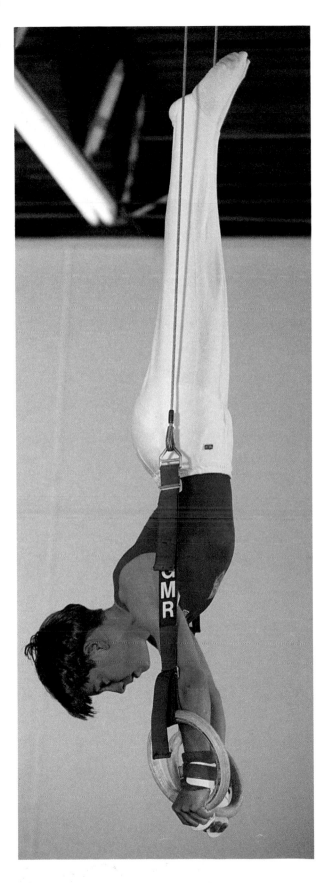

● *Still Rings*

The still rings are made of wood or fiberglass. The rings are about 1 foot, 7½ inches apart. They hang about 8 feet, 3 inches above the ground. A gymnast does circling and swinging movements.

Pat is doing a handstand at left. Nick, above, is demonstrating a back lever.

● *Parallel Bars*

The parallel bars are two wooden or fiberglass bars. They are 11 feet, 6 inches long and about 1½ feet apart. Two **uprights** hold the bars 5 feet, 6 inches above the ground.

A gymnast swings his body above and between the bars, as Tony is doing. The gymnast has to keep his routine flowing smoothly.

● *Horizontal Bar*

One of the most thrilling boys' events is the horizontal bar, or high bar. The horizontal bar is an 8-foot long steel bar. It is about 8 feet above the floor. The high bar is often lowered for beginning gymnasts.

Christian is doing a basic swing, called a **giant swing**. He holds onto the bar with both hands and swings his body around it. He keeps his body stretched out as he swings around the bar.

Girls' Events

● *Floor Exercise*

A floor exercise routine has tumbling and dance moves. The gymnast must match her moves to the music she has chosen. Her performance can't last more than 1½ minutes.

Sara is doing a **front walk-over**, below, as part of her routine. She performs with a straight, smooth body line.

A floor exercise routine also requires endurance. The last **tumbling pass** should be as difficult and exciting as the first.

● *Vault*

The girls' vault event is much like the boys' vault. The vaulting apparatus, or horse, is the same height—3 feet, 7 inches high. Girls and boys perform the same vaults. The girls' vault, however, is turned sideways.

Stacy is doing a vault. After she runs down the runway, she jumps onto the springboard.

Stacy touches the horse briefly with her hands. Then she pushes off the horse. She twists in the air during the postflight.

When she lands, Stacy tries to **stick** the landing. That means she tries to land without taking any steps to regain her balance.

Heidi injured her knee. After it healed, she began doing gymnastics again. She wears a brace to protect her knee from injury.

● *Uneven Parallel Bars*

The uneven parallel bars event combines the skill of the parallel bars with the thrill of the horizontal bar. The uneven parallel bars are two bars held up by steel uprights. The uneven parallel bars are the same length as the horizontal bar. One bar is 7 feet, 6 inches above the floor. The other bar is 4 feet, 11 inches.

A gymnast on the uneven parallel bars is always swinging and circling. Heidi is doing a giant swing.

• *Balance Beam*

A balance beam is made of wood or aluminum. It's covered with suede. The beam is 4 inches wide and 16 feet, 5 inches long. The beam is 3 feet, 11 inches above the floor for competition. It may be set lower for practice. A routine on the balance beam can't be longer than 1½ minutes. Timing begins when the gymnast's feet leave the floor in a **mount**. A **dismount** completes her routine.

Sara's **handstand**, at left, shows her balance. Gymnasts must also dance and tumble on the beam. Jill, below, is doing a back walkover.

Building Blocks

Learning to do gymnastics is like climbing up a ladder. Each skill builds on those the gymnast knows, just like each rung of a ladder leads to the next rung.

Not everyone learns at the same pace. Some gymnasts can go faster than others. Just as some people can race up a ladder by skipping rungs, some gymnasts can skip a few steps in the learning process. However, every gymnast must learn several key ideas.

First, a gymnast must know exactly where he or she is while in the air. A gymnast also must learn how to keep his or her body in the proper position. A gymnast's body flips and twists better if every part of the gymnast's body is in line.

Also, gymnasts must know how to fall without getting hurt. Everyone falls while learning skills. Knowing how to fall and how to land safely are important parts of doing gymnastics.

Other Equipment

Gymnasts need some special equipment to make their sport fun and safe. Landing mats are especially important. These mats go underneath the apparatus to protect the gymnast when he or she is doing a dismount. The mats are 4 to 10 inches high. Often, another 1-inch base mat is under the main mats.

Some gymnastics equipment can be changed to suit each gymnast's body size and strength. Coaches and gymnasts should check all the apparatus often to be sure each piece is stable, secure, and correctly set up.

Most gymnasts use chalk on their hands to help them get a good grip on the apparatus. Sometimes they use chalk on their feet too. The chalk helps keep hands and feet from getting sweaty.

*Many gymnasts also use **grips,** or handguards, when they are on the rings or any of the bars. The grips help to keep the gymnast's hands from getting blisters.*

There are three basic body positions a gymnast can use: **tuck, pike,** and **layout.** A gymnast's body moves best in the air when it's in one of these positions.

When Stacy's knees are tucked in and her body looks like a ball, she is in the tuck position. When gymnasts are first learning to flip in the air, they learn this position.

Next, gymnasts learn to perform with straight legs. A gymnast's body moves more slowly through the air when the gymnast's legs are straight.

In the pike position, at left, Stacy bends at the waist but keeps her legs straight. In the layout position, below, the gymnast's entire body is in a straight line.

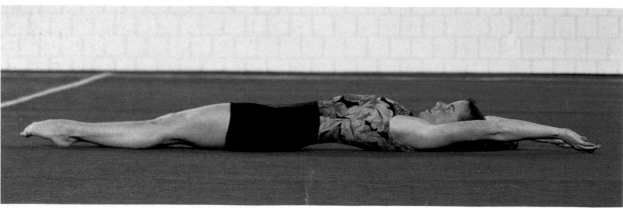

Gymnasts need flexible legs, backs, and shoulders. Adam is doing a **pancake**. That move shows the flexibility of his legs and back. Even ankle flexibility is important. In gymnastics, stretched ankles look better than flexed ankles.

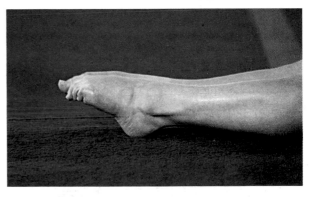

Gymnasts stretch their ankles and point their toes.

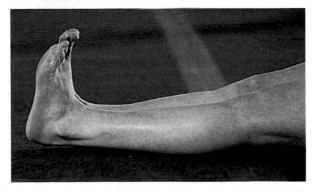

Gymnasts try not to bend their ankles while performing.

Gymnasts must also be strong. The uneven parallel bars for girls and the still rings for boys are two of the events that demand strength.

Gymnasts do exercises to build their strength. This is called conditioning. Sometimes practicing the basic skills of gymnastics is part of the conditioning sessions.

For example, Matt's **straddle** hold, at left, shows strength in his arms, legs, and abdomen. Below, Lori is doing push-ups, which develop arm strength.

Tumbling Basics

● *Handstand*

The handstand is an important skill that is used in many events. Mark, at left, is doing a handstand in his parallel bars routine. Lori's handstand, at right, shows her body in a perfectly straight line.

● *Roll*

The first gymnastics move many people learn is a **roll**. A roll can be performed forward or backward. Rolls can also be done on the balance beam.

Cathy moves her body from a stretched position to a small ball-like position. Once she is in

the tuck position, she rolls onto her rounded back. Her legs lift up and over her head.

Once Cathy's roll is completed, she stands up. She finishes with her body stretched toward the ceiling and her arms held high.

● *Cartwheel*

Gymnasts can tumble forward and backward. They can also tumble sideward. One fun way to tumble sideways is by doing a **cartwheel**.

Sara stands up straight with her arms reaching toward the ceiling. Then she lunges forward and turns sideways until her right hand touches the mat.

She kicks her legs into the air into a straddle position. Her legs remain straight throughout the cartwheel.

When she's upside down, Sara's body looks like the spokes of a wheel. Then her left foot lands on the mat, followed by her right foot. She ends in the same position as she started.

Left or Right?

How do you know which hand to put down first—your right or your left—when you're doing a cartwheel? Do you put down your right because you're right-handed? Not necessarily! When people write, they are naturally either right- or left-handed. People also are usually right- or left-side tumblers. You may write with your right hand, however, and prefer to do cartwheels with your left hand first!

Coaches often ask beginning gymnasts to learn the basic skills on both sides. That way, they learn to tumble to the left and to the right.

● *Roundoff*

A **roundoff** changes forward power into backward power. Lori begins her roundoff with a quick run into a **hurdle** or hop step. Then she reaches through the **lunge** position and puts down both hands at almost the same time. As she pushes

through her arms and chest, she brings her feet together. Her body rotates over her head when she is upside down. When she snaps down, she's facing the opposite direction from when she began. She ends with her hands held high.

● *Handspring*

Gymnasts can do handsprings going backward or forward. The **back handspring** is sometimes called a flip-flop or a flick-flack.

Beth pushes off her feet. She

leans backward and lands on her hands. She flips her body over her head and lands on her feet. Beth needs strength to boost her body high into the air.

Forward or Backward?

Some beginning gymnasts think it's easier to tumble forward than backward. When they tumble forward they can see where they're headed. But in a forward move, you can't see your feet land. When you land a backward skill, you can see your hands or your feet land. Think about landing on the balance beam.

● *Somersault*

People often call a **somersault** a "flip." Somersaults are fun to do. As you turn in the air, you will feel as if you're flying.

A somersault can be done backward, forward, or sideward. Often a gymnast will do a roundoff or a back handspring just before a somersault. Somersaults are used in floor exercise routines and for dismounts. A dismount is a skill done to leave an apparatus.

Pat is doing a front somersault. He lifts his arms. As his arms rise, Pat pushes off with

both feet up into the air. At the top of the lift, Pat tucks his body. He leans forward. His body rotates all the way around. Pat lands on both feet. His hands never touch the floor.

You can do a somersault in the tucked, piked, or layout position. If you are in the layout position, you can add a half, full, double-full, or even a triple-full twist. The somersault is truly an exciting move!

Dance

Dance is a big part of girls' floor exercise routines. Dance is also a big part of the balance beam event. In both events, the gymnast must do turns, jumps, and leaps. She should also use runs, walks, and skips. She needs to use her arms and body in graceful motions, such as **body waves**. Gymnasts spend almost as much time and effort learning dance skills as they do learning tumbling skills.

● *Turns*

Gymnasts do all turns on the toes and balls of their feet. A **pivot turn** is the most basic turn. Cathy starts facing in one direction. She is on her toes. She then twists, or pivots, to face the opposite direction.

l turn, Kristy begins
up her arms. She
rd onto the ball of
e closer her leg is to
her body, the faster she will turn.
She looks straight ahead and
twists on her base leg all the
way around.

She ends the full turn facing the same direction as when she started. She holds her arms in a graceful pose.

● *Jumps*

When a gymnast does a jump, she leaves the floor from both feet and then lands on both feet at the same time. While she is in the air, the gymnast's legs may be in many different positions. Sara, above, is doing a straddle jump. Kristy, at left, is doing a tuck jump.

● *Leaps*

To do a leap, a gymnast shifts her weight from one foot to the other as high as possible while in the air. Several leaps are often done in a row.

The **split leap** Jill is doing is the most basic leap. Her legs must be parallel with the floor and absolutely straight at the height of this leap.

Typical Workout

Gymnasts learn new skills, create their routines, and practice skills during a workout. Most workouts have a warm-up, rotations on apparatus, and a conditioning session.

● Warm-up

During the warm-up, gymnasts stretch, flex, and limber up their bodies. A warm-up is usually done on the floor mat. Sometimes gymnasts use the equipment to help them warm up.

● Apparatus Practice

After the warm-up, gymnasts divide into smaller groups to work on the apparatus. The time a gymnast spends on each piece of equipment is called a rotation. There should be at least one coach for eight gymnasts on an apparatus.

Most coaches want every gymnast to work out regularly on each piece of equipment. Working on different skills helps a gymnast become well-rounded and strong in many areas.

● Conditioning

After the rotations are done, it's time for conditioning. Gymnasts do push-ups, sit-ups, splits, and sprints to increase their strength, flexibility, and endurance.

SHOWTIME

Jill is waiting for the green flag. In a few seconds, she will be up on the balance beam. She will be flipping, turning, dancing, and leaping. Her coach whispers in her ear, "Do what you know you can do, Jill!"

There's the green flag. Jill raises her arms to **salute** the judge. And she's off!

For a minute and a half, Jill dances and tumbles on that skinny little piece of wood. The balance beam is her stage. When she's finished, her coach and teammates clap and cheer. Let's find out how you can get involved in competitive gymnastics too.

What Does a Coach Do?

A coach must be able to teach many skills for each piece of apparatus. A coach assists, or spots, all the moves his or her gymnasts do while learning. Most coaches are also trained in first aid.

A coach also needs to know about the mental aspects of gymnastics. For example, a coach must be able to help a gymnast who is afraid of trying a new skill.

As gymnasts grow up, changes in their bodies affect their ability to tumble. Most women are done with gymnastics meets by the time they are 20 years old. Men often stop competing when they are in their mid-20s. Some gymnasts love the sport so much that they become coaches. As coaches, they can stay involved in gymnastics.

Getting Started

Recreation centers and YMCAs often have gymnastics classes. Usually, however, those who want to be gymnasts take lessons at gymnastics clubs. Clubs usually give gymnasts the chance to compete against gymnasts from other clubs.

The United States Gymnastics Federation (USGF) runs gymnastics programs at the local, state, regional, and national levels. The USGF sets the rules for competition that all its member gymnasts and coaches must follow.

The lowest levels of the USGF program are used in school gym classes or noncompetitive programs. Competition begins in the middle levels. Gymnasts at these levels learn routines that they perform in meets.

In the advanced levels, gymnasts create their own routines. These routines must include

some of the specific skills that are defined in the **Code of Points**. The Code of Points is the rule book of the **International Gymnastics Federation**.

Gymnasts compete against other gymnasts of the same age and skill level. There are children's, junior, and senior age groups. The gymnasts you see on television in the Olympics have gone beyond these levels. They are called elite gymnasts.

Some gymnastics clubs compete against each other outside of the USGF system. Many junior and senior high schools sponsor teams. The schools and independent clubs use the National Federation of High School Gymnastics rule book instead of the Code of Points for their meets.

Getting Ready for a Meet

In USGF competition, a gymnast must compete in every event. He or she is called an all-arounder. Competing all-around is not required in independent club meets and for most school competitions. When a gymnast competes in just one or a few events, he or she is called a specialist.

Once a gymnast knows the basic skills, he or she must put them together into a series of moves. A gymnast's floor exercise routine should look as easy to perform at the end as it did at the beginning when the gymnast was full of energy. Both the floor exercise and balance beam events are timed. Gymnasts in these events must practice so that they don't perform their routine too quickly or too slowly.

Judging

Usually two judges watch each routine in each event. As many as four judges watch important competitions.

The judges look for a performance that is as close to perfection as possible. Each routine is judged on a 10.0 scale. A routine is worth 10 points if it is performed perfectly and includes all the required skills. The 10 points are awarded based on how difficult the skills are, how the routine flows, and how well the skills are performed. Points or tenths of a point are taken away for mistakes. Judges give bonus points to gymnasts for doing difficult skills that weren't required.

Routines must be original and exciting. Judges sometimes have different opinions. When the routine is scored by more than one judge, the final score is the average of the scores.

Mental Preparation

When you watch gymnastics, you may think, "How does she do that?" and "Won't he get hurt?" Gymnasts may be afraid or nervous about performing in front of an audience. When a gymnast is nervous, he or she is more likely to make mistakes that can lead to an injury. Or, a gymnast might feel a lot of pressure to perform well for teammates and fans. He or she might worry that a fall would cost his or her team a victory.

Good coaches help their gymnasts deal with these worries. Coaches spot, or physically assist, gymnasts. A coach won't let a gymnast do a move alone until he or she is confident the gymnast won't get hurt.

Coaches don't let a gymnast use a skill in a meet unless he or she has first practiced it many, many times. Some people say, "Practice makes perfect." Gymnastics coaches say, "Perfect practice makes perfect."

Sometimes coaches tell gymnasts to imagine doing their

routines perfectly before they go to sleep or right before they compete. Some gymnasts write in a journal. They write about their progress, problems, frustrations, and victories. Writing about their concerns helps some gymnasts feel better and worry less.

Safety First

Gymnasts need a safe environment in which to learn skills. The gymnasium should have modern equipment. There should be ample room in between pieces of equipment. Protective mats should cover the floor under and around the apparatus. A coach must know how to teach and spot all the skills a gymnast does. Coaches should also know first aid.

RAZZLE DAZZLE

Perhaps your goal is to compete in the Olympic Games. If it is, you will need to master some dazzling moves. Even if you don't plan on being an Olympian, you may want to try some advanced skills.

Ask your coach for help to learn more difficult moves. Remember to always have a spotter when you're working on new skills. And don't get discouraged. Difficult moves take time and effort to master. The results, however, are stunning.

Shannon Miller is a member of the United States national team. She knows many difficult moves and has great form.

Gymnasts often use somersaults in floor exercise routines. Stacy is demonstrating a back somersault.

Once a gymnast can do both front and back flips in the tuck position, he or she can add variations.

Beth shows one such variation below. She straightens and splits her legs to do a **layout stepout** back somersault.

In vaulting, advanced work also means adding twists or somersaults in the postflight.

There are advanced skills on both the boys' horizontal bar and the girls' uneven parallel bars. These skills often require that the gymnast let go of the

bar in mid-air and then grab it
again. Above, Sara has let go
of the uneven bars while doing
this counter.

The parallel bars event is unique to boys' gymnastics. Pat is demonstrating one spectacular move on the parallel bars. It's called a stütz. He swings his body through the bars and lets go of the bars with both hands. Then Pat twists and grabs the bars again. Now, he's facing the opposite direction.

Jill shows her body control and flexibility by performing a **needle scale** on the balance beam.

Tony is doing **scissors** in his pommel horse routine. He needs strength and accuracy for this move.

For her dismount off the balance beam, Kristy jumps into a back handspring. She lands back on the beam, and pushes

off again right away. Her momentum from the back hand-spring gives her back somer-sault dismount extra height.

Rhythmic gymnasts use balls, ribbons, and hoops.

Gymnastic Cousins

The six boys' and four girls' events described in this book are called artistic gymnastics. There are other kinds of gymnastics. Rhythmic gymnastics, acrogymnastics, and sports acrobatics aren't as well known as artistic gymnastics, but they are fun too.

Rhythmic gymnasts perform floor exercise routines. Their routines don't include tumbling moves. Instead, rhythmic gymnasts use a ribbon, ball, hoop, clubs, or rope. Trampoline, double mini-trampoline, synchronized trampoline, and power tumbling are acrogymnastics events. In sports acrobatics, pairs and groups of gymnasts perform. The gymnasts balance on their partners. Sometimes they somersault off their partners.

Gymnastics is a beautiful sport. Gymnasts try to perform their skills perfectly. They try to make their difficult moves look easy to do. Gymnasts also try to create new skills that dazzle their fans. Gymnastics constantly changes, but it will always be exciting to watch and fun to learn.

GYMNASTICS TALK

apparatus: The equipment used in the gymnastics events, specifically: uneven parallel bars, horizontal bar, rings, pommel horse, vault, parallel bars, and balance beam.

back handspring: A jump backward onto the hands, followed by a quick push from the hands to the feet. Also called flip-flop or flick-flack.

balance beam: A wooden or aluminum beam, 4 inches wide, 16 feet, 5 inches long, raised on metal supports 3 feet, 11 inches high. Girls perform timed routines on the beam.

body wave: A technique involving successive movements of the arms or the whole body.

cartwheel: A rotation of the gymnast's body sideways through the upside down position on the hands and onto the feet, landing one foot at a time with straight legs.

circles: A circular movement of one or both legs on the pommel horse.

Code of Points: The international rule book used for judging routines.

comaneci: A dismount from the uneven parallel bars performed by doing a circle off the top bar followed by a quarter twist and back flip.

dismount: A means of leaving the apparatus at the completion of a routine

floor exercise: A timed gymnastics event performed on a mat measuring 40 feet by 40 feet. Boys perform tumbling skills. Girls tumble and dance to music.

front handspring: A forward jump onto the gymnast's hands with immediate rotation forward onto his or her feet.

front walkover: A movement rotating forward round the shoulder axis, with momentary hand support in the upside down position.

full turn: A rotation about the vertical plane of the body in dance. In tumbling, a rotation about the horizontal axis.

giant swing: A skill used on the high bar and uneven parallel bars where the fully extended body circles around the bar.

grips: Devices gymnasts wear on their hands to hold onto the apparatus better. Also called handguards.

handstand: A move in which the gymnast supports his or her body on his or her hands while upside down.

horizontal bar: A metal bar supported by metal poles on which boys perform routines. Also called a high bar.

hurdle: A hop step used to begin a tumbling skill.

International Gymnastics Federation: The governing body of international gymnastics. Also known as FIG after its French translation.

layout: The basic body position in which the gymnast's body is completely stretched out and extended.

layout stepout: A back somersault with the gymnast's legs split and extended.

lunge: A leaning-over position with one foot ahead of the other and the gymnast's weight mainly on his or her lead leg, which is bent.

mount: A method of getting onto the apparatus to start a routine.

needle scale: A balance pose used on the balance beam in which one leg supports the gymnast's body and the other points to the ceiling.

pancake: A body position in which the gymnast's upper body is piked over flat to his or her lower body.

parallel bars: A pair of wooden or fiberglass bars of the same height and parallel to each other which are supported by adjustable metal poles. Also called P-bars.

pike: A basic body position in which the gymnast's body is folded at the hips. The gymnast's arms and legs are held straight.

pivot turn: A half-turn on the balls of both feet.

pommel horse: A leather-covered wooden frame with a straight body and two handles, called pommels, screwed into it. Also called a side horse.

postflight: A phase of the vault during which the gymnast's body is in space, from the time the gymnast's hands leave the horse until his or her feet land on the mat.

preflight: A phase of the vault during which the gymnast's body is in space, from the time his or her feet leave the board until the gymnast's hands touch the horse.

rings: A pair of stationary rings supported from ropes and straps. Also called still rings.

Nikki demonstrates a scale on the balance beam. This pose requires balance and control. Beam routines must show both qualities.

roll: A tucked position moving either forward or backward during which the gymnast starts and ends on his or her feet.

roundoff: A cartwheel variation in which the gymnast lands on both feet at the same time, facing the way he or she began.

salute: An arm signal by a gymnast to a judge that indicates that the gymnast is ready to begin his or her routine.

scissors: A move used on the pommel horse in which the legs extend and cross each other.

somersault: A 360-degree rotation of the gymnast's body about its horizontal axis with upward flight and without hand support. Also called a flip or salto or somi.

split leap: A dance skill in which the gymnast pushes off of one foot and transfers her weight from one leg to the other with both legs parallel to the floor at the height of the leap.

spring floor: A type of floor exercise mat made with springs or foam blocks, wooden boards, a foam pad, and carpeting.

stick: The action of landing a dismount without taking a step or completing a beam routine without any falls.

straddle: A body position of straight legs held apart with a wide angle between them.

tsukahara: A type of vault in which the gymnast does a quarter or half twist onto the horse followed by a one and a-half back flip off.

tuck: The basic body position in which the gymnast's knees are bent up to his or her chest, which is rounded, and the gymnast's chin is in and down.

tumbling pass: A series of tumbling skills on the floor exercise event.

twist: To rotate about the body's vertical axis.

uneven parallel bars: A pair of wooden or fiberglass bars on metal supports. The bars are parallel to each other but one is higher than the other. Also called asymmetric bars.

uprights: The vertical poles that support the parallel and uneven parallel bars.

vault: A flat-surfaced, leather-covered rectangular structure on wooden supports. Also called a horse.

FURTHER READING

Conner, Bart. *Winning the Gold*. New York: Warner Books, Inc., 1985.

Feeney, Rik. *Gymnastics: A Guide for Parents and Athletes*. Indianapolis, Ind.: Masters Press, 1992.

Goodbody, John. *The Illustrated History of Gymnastics*. London: Stanley Paul & Co., Ltd., 1982.

Krementez, Jill. *A Very Young Gymnast*. New York: Alfred A. Knopf, Inc., 1980.

Mulvihill, Dick and David Day. *The Show Me Gymnastics Series*. Atlanta, Ga.: Linton Day Publishing Company, 1990.

Whitlock, Steve. *Make the Team: Gymnastics for Girls*. Boston, Mass.: The Time Inc. Magazine Company (Little, Brown and Company), 1991.

FOR FURTHER INFORMATION

International Gymnast Magazine
   (published monthly except bimonthly
   June/July and August/September)
P. O. Box 2450
Oceanside, CA 92051

International Gymnastics Hall of Fame
227 Brooks Street
Oceanside, CA 92054

United States Gymnastics Federation
201 S. Capital Suite 300
Pan Am Plaza
Indianapolis, IN 46225

INDEX